T0167205

Emanations from the Corpse of
Little Burgundy

Emanations from the Corpse of Little Burgundy

By

Tom Massiah

Order this book online at www.trafford.com
or email orders@trafford.com

Most Trafford titles are also available at major online book retailers.

Printed in the United States of America.

ISBN: 978-1-4669-4975-1 (sc)
ISBN: 978-1-4669-4974-4 (e)

Trafford rev. 07/26/2012

 www.trafford.com

North America & international
toll-free: 1 888 232 4444 (USA & Canada)
phone: 250 383 6864 ♦ fax: 812 355 4082

DEDICATION

I dedicate this mini-novel to my wife Clemmie, who has patiently put up with my imperfections during just over 60 years of marriage to date. And I would also like to thank my daughter Sharleen for providing the impetus for this undertaking, by her repeated requests to me, that I tell about my experiences growing up in Little Burgundy.

CONTENTS

ACKNOWLEDGEMENTS

I want to acknowledge and thank my friend Richard Da Costa for undertaking to format not only this novel, but also for having done similarly with my autobiography **Musings Of A Native Son**, (ISBN 141201809-9) several years ago. In doing so, he undertook a Herculean task, in both instances, with diligence and expertise. He has proven to be more like a brother, than like a friend.

Nevertheless, I want to dedicate a poem on friendship (that I wrote several years ago) to him, who has been a true friend to me.

Thoughts On A True Friend
by
Tom Massiah

You are truly blessed—if you
have one true friend,
Someone who stands by you—
right to the end;
Someone who knows and accepts
all your faults,
Yet never condemns you—nor
verbally assaults.
Your friend is your confidant—
your constant resource,
In times of rejoicing—in times of remorse.
It matters not how others may rate—
or berate you,
True friends are straightforward—
they're never askew!
The house that you live in—the
car that you drive,

The trappings and status for which
most of us strive.
These things may matter—only
while you're alive;
But when the 'grim reaper' comes—
in all of his stealth,
He won't let you pack either jewels
or wealth.
For your only portable at life's very end,
Is the enduring approval—of one
true friend.

PREFACE

The impetus for culling the various stories which comprise this brief history of Little Burgundy is the repeated requests from my daughter Sharleen, that I undertake such a task. In 2004, I wrote and published my autobiography **Musings Of A Native Son**. But that undertaking dealt exclusively with 70 years of my life, and did not involve any of the characters or incidents elaborated on in the present work. So in this writing, I am adopting the posture of a reporter, who wants to share with his readers, some of the things that he experienced as a resident of Little Burgundy.

The place that was known as Little Burgundy no longer exists, having either disappeared altogether, or being changed through gentrification, especially in the area of the ancient Atwater Market. It was the focal area of working-class Blacks. But most Blacks have left the area, and have been replaced by immigrants primarily from Asia.

I hope that those of you who never lived there, will nevertheless find the stories latently interesting. And for former residents, I hope that you will enjoy these reminiscences as much as I did, in writing about them.

Thomas Massiah

Chapter 1

THE SITE

It is fitting that I provide the reader with information as to the origin of the name Little Burgundy. The name derives from an area in the Southwest borough of the city of Montreal known in French as La Petite-Bourgogne, later anglicized (near the turn of the 20th century) to its better known name.

Strangely, the part of Montreal that I am about to describe, consists of only some eight streets (Peel to Richmond Square), from East to West. It is bounded by St. Antoine St. on the North side, and St. Jacques St. on the South. And it was situated in Montreal's Ste. Cunegonde ward.[*Actually, the official geographic borders of this area are much larger than what I have chosen to write about*.] Yet in this predominantly Black microcosm (designated years ago as 'Little Burgundy'), one could find as many odd-ball characters, as were portrayed by Damon Runyon, in his many vignettes of New York City.

I lived there for 13 years (1938-1951), and was able to observe these hard-to-believe characters, and their daily machinations—as their lives unfolded—in this cauldron of humanity. Our family resided at 1500 St. Antoine St.—at the corner of Lusignan St. We occupied the second and third floors of a three storey house, which we rented from a kindly butcher, Gustave Deslauriers—who had a stall in the Atwater market.

The first floor was rented by Branch #50, of the Canadian Legion. This branch consisted entirely of Black veterans of World War I. They ran the branch as a 'watering hole', with booze, music and licentious behaviour lasting until 2-3am—seven days a week. And no amount of pleading by my widowed mother (for a cessation of the noise and other objectionable activities), had any effect. These legionnaires and their women—many of whom were white—continued their hedonistic revelry unabated. So to this day, I have a very unfavourable opinion of legionnaires in general, based on my 13 years observance of what went on at Branch # 50 of the Legion. And I have steadfastly refused to either buy or wear a poppy, when I see them being sold just prior to Remembrance Day, November 11 of each year, since 1918. I have continued to do so, even though my late older brother (James) served overseas in The Canadian Army, during World War II.

Perhaps the most prominent businesses in Little Burgundy were two night clubs—Rockhead's (at the Southeast corner of Mountain and St. Antoine Sts.) and the Ste.

Michel Cabaret, situated on the West side of Mountain St., just below St. Antoine St. to the North, and Torrence St. to the South.

Rockhead's was owned by Rufus Rockhead, who was born in Jamaica. He was the boss, and he ran his establishment with an iron fist—for what seemed like an eternity. His nightclub consisted of only two floors, with a tavern downstairs. And he neglected to buy some property just to the South of him, when it became available for sale. So thereafter, he was prevented from expanding his facilities—even had he wanted to do so. Yet, despite the sparseness of space at Rockhead's, it was the cabaret of choice in Montreal, during the late 1940s and early 1950s. Many of the patrons were dowager white women (from affluent Westmount), who came seeking an evening's involvement with some of the black 'bucks' who also patronized Rockhead's. And many prominent white men also patronized Rockhead's, whenever they felt inclined to 'slumming' for an evening. Throughout, Rufus could be seen—impeccably attired (with a rose in his jacket's lapel), and always near to the entrance of his nightclub—imploring the patrons to sit down and be quiet! His favourite request was '. . . . Sit down! Sit down on your ass, s'il vous plaît!'

Diagonally across the street from Rockhead's was the Ste. Michel nightclub. Although, like Rockhead's it was also a cabaret, it seemed less so, on at least two counts:—1) the calibre of its' shows and 2.) its décor and clientele. Whereas Rockhead's featured its cabaret, the Ste. Michel seemed to feature its' downstairs' bar. There you could buy a quart of beer for $0.75, and listen to endless one-chord piano renditions by a pianist, named Roy. However, over the years, many up and coming musicians used the Ste Michel bar as their launching pad. They were trumpet players, trombonists, drummers, bassists and even jazz-violinists. Another thing which came to characterize the Ste. Michel bar, was the very late-night jam sessions that were held there. In the late 1940s (and usually after 3 a.m. on Saturday), jazz musicians from nightclubs all over Montreal, would congregate in the Ste Michel bar for a jam session. And these sessions would last until 7 or 8a.m. on Saturday.

There was one memorable period during Rufus Rockhead's ownership of his cabaret, that he showed how inflexible he was business-wise. The story goes that he was approached by a representative of the Union Nationale government, informing him that the Ste Michel Cabaret had contributed $20,000 to their campaign fund. The implication was—do likewise, or else! Apparently, Rufus refused to comply, so he was promptly closed down for something like 11 years. Now, as far as I could discern, Rufus' refusal to pay the bribe demanded by the Union Nationale government, was not based on some lofty moral principal held by him. Rather it seemed to be either simply parsimony or pig-headedness, on his part. Either way, it showed that he had a serious deficiency in understanding how the entertainment business was conducted in Quebec in those days. And illustrative of his character—when Rufus was finally re-licensed 11 years later—he re-opened with the same show that he closed with, 11 years earlier!

Another of the businesses (in the same block where Rockhead's Paradise was situated) was a poolroom, operated by a chap named Howie. He was born in Truro, Nova Scotia, but had been brought to Montreal (by his parents) years earlier, when they opened their poolroom on St. Antoine St., in Little Burgundy. Howie was one of the most unforgettable characters (among the many characters) that you would encounter there. I am sure that if he was alive today, videos would have been made of his numerous antics. Whenever business got slow in the poolroom, Howie would undertake to regale those of us who were present, either by making fun of one of the patrons, or by telling us of some hilarious thing that took place among some unnamed blacks in his native city, Truro. Or, he would simply select someone in the poolroom to be the butt of the joke or prank that he was about to portray. Let me give you an example.

One afternoon, around 3p.m., several of us were sitting around in Howie's poolroom, when he selected a youngster who was about 17 or 18 years old, and was a stranger to the rest of us. Howie asked him, when had he arrived in town? The youngster replied '. . . . around 3 p.m.!'. Howe's rejoinder was '. . . . I didn't know that freight trains arrived in town that late!', implying that the youngster was a hobo. Then he continued his lampooning of his chosen 'victim for mockery', by asking him what he had had for breakfast that day. And before he could reply, Howie said to him '. . . I would give you some food to eat, but I'm afraid that good food would kill you. You look like you've been raised on corn flakes, and seem like starvation to me!'

Those of us who were present literally rolled over with laughter at Howie's put down of his latest victim. And thereafter this youngster was known as 'Starvation', even though he had a perfectly good name, Stewart.

Now, I hope that I have not conveyed the idea that Howie's lampooning was mean-spirited, because it was not. Rather it was simply his way of infusing some hilarity into the otherwise dour atmosphere of his poolroom, which was always in need of a good sprucing up, both materially and atmospherically.

The other poolroom in Little Burgundy was owned by an Italian gentleman named Paul Di Carlo. It was situated on the North side of St. Antoine, between Guy and Richmond Square. When I was about 16 years of age, I had an obsession with pool, and frequented Di Carlo's poolroom regularly. But my mother was determined that neither me nor my younger brother Michael were to patronize Paul's poolroom. So unannounced she would visit the poolroom, brandishing a strap. And not only did she trash us if she found us there, but she also threatened Paul that she would have his poolroom closed, for catering to under—age youngsters. So reluctantly, Paul barred Michael and me from his poolroom. Curiously, today, I live in a condominium which has a first-rate poolroom in the recreation centre. And I have a stylish pool cue, given me by my wife Clemmie. But I can't tell you the last time that I played a game of pool in our condo's poolroom. Obviously, one's interests change with time.

There were a number of other small businesses near to Rockhead's and the St. Michel cabarets. These included The Boston Café, The Snack Shop, Nathan's Delicatessen, Jim Ball's Barber Shop and Ben White's General Store. Each had a unique way of contributing to the atmosphere that characterized 'Little Burgundy' in those days. So let me tell you something about each of these establishments, and their impact on the neighbourhood.

Ben Wilson (from Detroit, Michigan) and Clara Pelly Wilson (from Antigonish, Nova Scotia) purchased the Boston Café in the early 1920s. It was located on St. Antoine St., just a bit East of Rockhead's Paradise. One of their early employees was Ethel Walters (from Bangor, Maine), who was Clara's niece. She worked for her Aunt (in the Boston Café) for several years, serving its customers southern style nutritious meals at affordable prices. In 1933, Ethel married John Madison (a native of Dresden, Ontario). And in 1940, they opened a restaurant of their own, called The Snack Shop, on St. Antoine St. (just West of Mountain St), and approximately two blocks from the Boston Café. As its name indicated, snacks were the type of meals provided in the Madison's restaurant, in contrast to the cuisine served in the Wilson's establishment. However, what characterized both of these restaurants is that, throughout their existence (under these owners), there was never anything raucous or illegal occurring in either of these businesses.

Another of the businesses in Little Burgundy was Nathan's Delicatessen. It was located on Mountain St., slightly north of the Ste. Michel Cabaret. What characterized Nathan's was that he introduced Smoked Meat sandwiches to downtown Montreal. Prior to that, this delicacy was available initially only at Ben's, which was located on Burnside St. (near to the Mount Royal Hotel) in uptown Montreal. Nathan's wife presided over the sale of their principal deli item 'smoked meat', all the time showing her undisguised loathing of her black clientele. She and Nathan had two daughters, who were not among the most beautiful women that I have ever seen. But I am confident that Mrs. Nathan (I never got to know their family name) would have had a stroke if either of her daughters deigned to even look at one of the black males, who patronized their business. However, two things kept us buying smoked meat sandwiches from Nathan's. The first was the price. Nathan's charged $0.20 a sandwich, while at Ben's it cost $0.50. And Nathan's was close at hand—and downtown, whereas Ben's required that you go uptown, and pay considerably more, for essentially the same sandwich.

Another of Little Burgundy's businesses was the Snack Shop. The Madisons had sold it to Knobby Clarke (a rather loquacious WWII veteran from the West Indies), in the late 1940s. He had a very different idea as to what constituted a 'snack' and what was a 'meal'. So his 'snacks' were essentially full-blown West Indian meals. This conspired against the success of his business, as most of his 'snacks' had to be consumed around the normal 12:00 noon to 2:00p.m. lunchtime. Eventually, other actual snack shops opened in the vicinity, and Knobby's business had to close. But before I write it off, as just another passing venture, let me tell you a little more about its character.

As I said earlier, Knobby was talkative. And being a WWII veteran who had served overseas in Italy, he was not averse to spinning exaggerated tales of his exploits there. I recall on story that he told about his encounter with a Colonel, whom he said wanted to post him to Toronto! What he actually meant was Taranto (Italy). But for the life of him, he kept calling the place Toronto! Nevertheless, he (a buck private) insisted that he defied the Colonel, by refusing his order to deploy to Toronto! Such was the kind of constant hyperbole that one would encounter in Knobby's Snack Shop.

Unlike the Boston Café, where clientele ate their meal and left, there was a great deal of loitering in Knobby's Snack Shop. Perhaps this was due to the seating, which consisted of some 8 or so counter-stools, augmented by 2or 3 small chair and table sets. Hyperbole and stupid talk were hallmarks of conversation in the Snack Shop, and the 'n-word' was almost sacrosanct there. It seemed that it gave its user (who was black) a sense of being significantly uplifted, whenever he used it to demean the one towards whom he directed it. I remember having the 'n-word' directed at me one day in the Snack Shop, by a chap named Lou Diamond, as I sat on one of the counter stools, with my back to the counter. He came in, and walked over both of my feet, without saying a word. I called out to him saying '. . . Hey Lou, you can walk on the top of my feet; I'll try to get along using the bottom!'. He replied '. . . Oh Nigger, if your feet weren't out there, they wouldn't be stepped on!' With that, I informed him that my feet would still be there when he would be ready to leave, and invited him to step on them again. He never did. That was part of the bravura and intimidation extant in the Snack Shop (and its environs) at the time. If you succumbed to it once, you would be victimized forever thereafter.

Another of the small businesses in Little Burgundy was a groceteria owned by a Jamaican named Ben White. It was situated on Aqueduct St., just South of St. Antoine St., and close to Torrance St. Ben was an extremely cordial and ambitious businessman. He was always trying to provide a good life for his three children. So he enrolled his two sons in the local YMCA, and enrolled his daughter in the YWCA. All three of his children became outstanding swimmers. But none of them achieved the academic stature that their father had hoped for them. Nor did they continue the business, once their father passed on. So all that can be said about this little groceteria is that it existed there—once upon a time.

Perhaps the most celebrated non-black-owned restaurant in Little Burgundy was the Greek-owned restaurant Papadakis, situated at the Southeast corner of Windsor and St. Antoine St. For some unknown reason, it was our custom to assemble there at around 3a.m. Sunday, to down a grilled cheese sandwich. Don't ask me why we were always ready to eat a grilled cheese sandwich at such an ungodly hour, but we did so for years! Then, afterwards, invariably we made our way to our respective homes. There was nothing spectacular about the place, but it seemed to have an attraction that enticed its patrons.

There were three black barbers in Little Burgundy—Bob Alleyne, Jim Ball and Dan Mayfield.

Bob (who was the most loquacious) was born in Barbados. He had served in World War I, and spent much of his time describing the locale of the Allied and German troop trench positions, while cutting his clients' hair. Invariably, this resulted in that client receiving a catastrophically bad haircut. His barbershop was situated on St. James St., between Dominion and Fulford St.—now Boulevard Georges—Vanier. Those of us who patronized him were so entranced with his tall tales of WWI, that we oftentimes purposely missed our turn to have our hair cut, so that we could hear more of his recollections. But he was anything but a skilled barber. In fact, he did such a poor job of cutting his godson's hair, that his godson's wife refused to speak to him for nearly a week, until some of his hair had re-grown on his head.

Jim Ball was a much quieter person than Bob Alleyne. And I never found out which West Indian island he came from. His barbershop was on St. Antoine St., near to St. Felix St. On each of the several times that he cut my hair, he did so without say more than a few words to me, or to anyone else. But on one occasion, a white woman made some enticing remarks to Jim. With that, he stopped cutting my hair, and disappeared into a room behind his barbershop. I heard the young lady pleading vainly to Jim, that he desist. But he did not. Shortly thereafter he emerged from the room, and proceeded to cut my hair, without uttering a single word. The look of satisfaction on his face said all that needed to be said.

Dan Mayfield was, in my view, the best barber of the three. However, before he became a barber, he played a tuba in Myron Sutton's band. His barbershop was within his dwelling, on the 2nd floor, directly above a Chinese restaurant, on the East side of Mountain St., near to St. Antoine St. The property was owned by Rufus Rockhead.

Dan was married to a white lady, who interrupted him constantly, while he was trying to cut hair. She was always in need of something. But I never saw Dan show annoyance over her interruptions. Instead he just acceded to her requests. Then he would resume cutting your hair.

As I said earlier, I felt that Dan was the best barber of the three. Why? Because, once when Dan was on holiday, I had my hair cut by a white French-Canadian barber. The result was a disaster, because he had no idea as to how to cut a black person's hair. So I had to wait until Dan returned from his vacation, to have him rectify the damage done to my hair by that white barber. At the time, it was well known that with the exception of Italian barbers, white barbers could not cut a black man's hair.

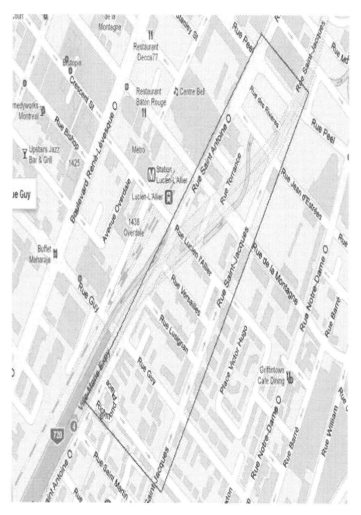

Approximate area of Little Burgundy

Chapter 2

THE WAR YEARS—1939 TO 1945

Oddly, World War II imposed a somewhat strange role on me. I will elaborate. I had just turned 13 when the conflict in Europe began, in September 1939. And my mother's youngest brother Uncle Tom came to Montreal, as part of a contingent of Black volunteers from the Caribbean island of Montserrat. They had opted to join the Canadian (rather the British) army, because the service pay was higher in the Canadian army. Somehow, I became the person who took these volunteer soldiers to two places. The first was to the West Indian Trade—Commissioner's Office on Ste. Sacrement St. in Montreal. His name was Mr. Dumaret, who was acting for the Trade-Commissioner, Mr. Rex Stollemeyer. And the second place was the Military District #4 Induction Office on St. James St., near to Windsor St. The visit to Mr. Dumaret's office was somewhat a 'pro forma' thing. But the induction into the Canadian army was the real deal. It involved the recruit getting an injection, which was always painful, and at times was also somewhat debilitating. But within a week or so, the recruits melded smoothly into army life. Most of the initial contingent joined the Royal Canadian Signal Corps, and were shipped to Kingston, Ontario to begin their training.

What happened to that first contingent of Caribbean volunteers was repeated with each contingent throughout the war, and for some reason that I do not understand to this day, I was always the one who took the new recruits to the army-induction process. In retrospect, I functioned not unlike the Judas steer at an abattoir!

Looking back, I feel that blacks (both male and female) participated fully in Canada's War effort. Even my older brother James (who was initially a most reluctant soldier) was ultimately persuaded to join the army, through a succession of maneuvers on the part of army officials. One of their favourite devices was to subject all reluctant recruits to virtually endless latrine—digging and tending duty. Eventually the ploy worked, and voila Canada had another 'volunteer' soldier! My brother James served overseas in North Africa and Italy, after a brief stay in the UK. He served with the New Westminister regiment.

There were so many other blacks who served primarily in the Canadian army during World War II, that it is difficult to decide who to mention. So I am going to invoke an author's prerogative, and select some at random. The first person who comes to mind is a friend who was just slightly older than I was at that time. His name was Bobby Thomas. We used to call him '. . . Bobby Tommy tough guy . . . '. But I can't think of a more inappropriate moniker, because Bobby was anything but tough. In fact, I would say unhesitatingly that he was one of the nicest individuals that I have ever met. Repeatedly, he told me that he wanted to join the Canadian army. And repeatedly, I tried to dissuade him from doing so. But eventually he did join the army, and soon he was shipped overseas. Regretfully, Bobby never returned to Canada. He was killed overseas. I think that it was either in Germany, or one of the neighbouring countries. I was devastated with the news of his death, and I continue to miss him even to this day.

Another war casualty was a chap named Clarence Trimm. One of his characteristics was that he would grasp his abdomen (almost convulsively) whenever he laughed. Well, almost paradoxically, the report is that he was killed by being shot in the abdomen. I was deeply touched by Clarence's untimely death (as a war casualty), because I felt that life owed him a lot more than he had received up till then.

For the most part, the majority of the Caribbean volunteers from Montserrat and Antigua returned safely after being sent overseas. But to my knowledge two did not return. They are Ben Allen and Wally Wade, both from the island of Montserrat.

There were other reluctant black volunteers, who joined the army, precisely because they were sure that they would be rejected. One of them, who I will call Lannie was noted for being always immaculate in his army uniform. In fact he was so much so, that a Brigadier-General asked him to be his batman. He declined, exclaiming '. . . *How can I keep you looking sharp, when I have to spend all my time trying to keep me looking Sharp?*'. So the Brigadier never got him as his batman, and Lannie continued his army-evading machinations. Eventually, he did succeed in getting out of the army without ever going overseas.

But the champion army—evader was a chap named Roy, who was actually in the Canadian army, yet spent every day AWOL. I don't know how he did it, because every day he wore his army uniform, yet he never showed up on parade. And somehow the military police (who made regular visits to Little Burgundy) never seemed to catch up with him. Roy was always clearly in sight, but somehow he always evaded being apprehended.

I hope that in presenting a few examples of black men who were reluctant inductees into the Canadian army, that I did not convey the idea that as a group, they were averse to serving in Canada's hour of need. Nothing could be further from the truth. Black men and women enlisted in the armed services fully proportionate to our numbers population-wise. However, it should be noted that during World War II, blacks were rigorously excluded from serving in Canada's navy, and we were only allowed to serve as ground-crew in the Royal

Canadian Air-Force. Contrast this with the fact that Caribbean blacks were permitted to serve as air-crew in the Royal Air-Force. And many went on to become pilots, navigators and bombardiers in the RAF. So the reason(s) for this discriminatory behaviour on the part of Canada's Naval and Air-Force hierarchy, remains an unexplained mystery to this day.

Three people whom I knew quite well, served as ground crew in the RCAF. They were Henry Langdon, Erwin Phillips and his cousin Freddy Phillips. Unfortunately, Erwin became a war casualty. But both Henry and Freddy survived the War, to go on to productive lives after being demobilized. Freddy, who became one of my closest friends, was the first black lawyer to be called to the Quebec Bar. He practiced Law in Montreal for a number of years, but has now retired from the practice.

Some of the blacks who had served in the Canadian armed forces took advantage of the opportunity offered them to further their education. In the next chapter, I will mention the names of those whom I knew best, who availed themselves of this opportunity. But regrettably, not everyone who could have benefited (by seizing this option) did so.

Chapter 3

SINNERS AND SAINTS

How one chooses whom to designate by which appellation, is of course arbitrary, given the number of characters from which to choose. So I am just going to describe as many of them as I can recall, and will leave it to the reader to designate them accordingly.

One chap who comes to mind was nicknamed 'the Horse'. His actual surname was Mapp, and I believe he came from the West Indian island of Barbados. He was a reasonably good housepainter when he was sober (which was a rarity), and he frequented Howie's poolroom. He was a devastating puncher, especially with his left hand, and he became particularly pugnacious whenever he drank. His favourite drink was beer. He would take a full quart bottle of beer, invert it into his mouth, and start emptying it in giant guzzles. It was quite a sight to watch the head of beer as the bottle's contents gradually disappeared into his mouth. When the beer bottle was empty, he might start on another. Or, he might become poetic. One of his favourite poetic utterances was:

The breeze may kiss the leaves as it passes by,
The singing birds may kiss the sky.
The dew may kiss the sleeping grass,
But you my friend . . . .
farewell!

Sometimes he would start to feel sorry for himself, and looking at the empty beer bottle would say '. . . . **you made me what I am today, you wine bastard!**', even though it was beer that he had been drinking.

But while drinking was his main activity, fighting was his avocation. Whenever he undertook to fight, he would circle his opponent with his left hand cocked menacingly. At the opportune moment, he would say **'here t is!'**, and with that, unleash what was usually a devastating, fight-ending blow to his opponent's jaw. In his younger years, there were few males who could stand up to him, but later on, his fighting prowess declined, and he began to lose fights as he got older. But indeed he was an unforgettable character.

What I have also been trying to portray, is the physical picture of the unspectacular locale that comprised Little Burgundy. Yet, despite its unprepossessing daytime topography, it had a night-time magnetism that is almost impossible to comprehend. This magnetism was undoubtedly due primarily to the unbelievable characters that comprised the persona of this part of Montreal. Let me tell you about some of them.

The Horse' was not the only boxer that one would meet in Little Burgundy back then. In fact it seemed that nearly everyone wanted to be a boxer. And some became quite good at it. The oldest was a chap called Jack Ward, who I am told was a sparring partner of Jack Johnson, the former Heavyweight Champion of the world in the 1920s. His nose had been broken, and permanently twisted to one side, as a result of one of Johnson's blows. And another was a former boxer named Charley Clay, who was blind, as a result of his days in the ring. If he got into a fight, and especially at night,—he would pull the light out from the ceiling,—so that both he and his opponent would be in the dark! But there were many other younger boxers, who frequented the neighbourhood. It seemed that at that time, every male and his brother wanted to be a boxer. But almost by default, there were many called, but few chosen. Arbitrarily I'll tell you about three of the better black boxers who frequented Little Burgundy at the time. They were Al Evans, Ralph Walton and Danny Webb.

Al was a very competent light-heavy weight, who came from Atlantic Canada, but later resided in 'Little Burgundy'. As an amateur, he trained at the Crescent Athletic Club, situated on St. Catherine St., near to St. Matthew St. In time, he turned professional, and compiled an impressive record of victories, fighting mostly in the New England states, primarily in cities such as Fall River, Massachusetts, and Bangor, Maine. So, although he was not an aggressive person out of the ring, he became someone that no one in his right mind would want to mess with! But one night I saw someone (who apparently had never heard of Al Evans) make him back down.

That evening there was a so-called 'nowhere' bus tour scheduled to depart from

Mountain and St. Antoine Sts. The bus began to fill up, and Al Evans' girlfriend sat in one of the 2-person seats alone. As I recall she was quite an attractive woman. A ruggedly built man, whom I had never seen before (or subsequently) boarded the bus, and sat down beside Al's girlfriend. But I do not recall him making any untoward advances towards her. Subsequently, Al boarded the bus, and walked to where his lady-friend, and the man were seated. Al said to the man '. . . . Nigger get out of that seat, or I'll punch you out!'. The man looked up at Al, sucked his tongue disdainfully, and said '. . . I can move two like you!' Now, earlier I had described the man as being ruggedly built. No. Although he was not extraordinarily tall, otherwise he was massive, and especially in his thighs! And I would guess that it would take someone with the power of a bulldozer in his hands, to knock this man off his feet. Without saying another word, Al Evans (the professional boxer) proceeded to the back of the bus, took a seat, and remained there until the bus reached its 'nowhere' destination (which was Plage Laval). In retrospect, I feel that Al had made a wise decision. Because, based on my cursory survey of that unknown man's physique, I haven't the slightest doubt that indeed, he could have made good on his threat 'to move two Als!'.

Another encounter between a professional boxer and a non-boxer, took place between Ralph Walton and a fellow named René Germaine. Like Al Evans, Ralph started his professional career in Montreal, but later on, he campaigned primarily in the New England States. In fact, one year he was so active that he fought 58 times! And not all of his opponents were no-bodies. For instance, in 1945 he fought and lost a 10-round bout to the Featherweight Champion Willie Pep, who was eventually elected to boxing's Hall of Fame in 1963. Initially Ralph fought as a lightweight, but later he fought as a welterweight.

Unlike Ralph, René wasn't a boxer. But he was someone that even an ex-professional wrestler (Joe Devalteau, who later joined the Montreal Police Force) steered clear of. He was not very tall (about 5ft.10in.), but he had probably a 19 inch neck. And he weighed about 220 pounds. His parents were from one of the French West Indian islands (i.e. either Guadeloupe or Martinique) and he lived in the near East part of Montreal—right in the heart of what was then the red-light district. However, whenever he came down to 'Little Burgundy', he did so quietly and unobtrusively. Nobody messed with him, and he troubled no-one. So it was surprising that once, he and Ralph Walton got into a physical conflict. It took place at the U.N.I.A.(i.e. Universal Negro Improvement Association) Hall, on Fulford St. (now called Boulevard Georges-Vanier) near to Rue. St. Jacques. So here is what took place.

Some 200 or so people had assembled in the 3rd floor of the U.N.I.A. hall, for a social function there. Suddenly, an altercation broke out between Ralph and René. I saw Ralph unleash a volley of punches at René. Instantly, René pinioned both of Ralph's arms to his sides, picked him up, ran across the room with him, and reared back, preparatory to throwing Ralph out of the 3rd floor window! At precisely that moment, René's brother Henri (who was substantially bigger than René) delivered three enormous punches to René's jaw, thereby stopping René in his tracks. Now, I should point out that, while René was a frequent visitor to Little Burgundy, Henri seldom did. So it was a fortunate happenstance for Ralph, that Henri had made one of his infrequent visits. For had he not been there, minimally, Ralph would have been seriously injured, or perhaps even killed, as a result of falling three stories, to the pavement below.

The other boxer that I would like to tell you about is Danny Webb. Like Al Evans, Danny started his career at the Crescent AC, boxing as a bantamweight. He was a very fast and superb boxer. One day during one of his training sessions, I talked him into taking on Johnny Greco, who was knocking out nearly all of his opponents, since his days as a paperweight fighter. Greco never laid a glove on Danny, during the three rounds they sparred! But years later, they would meet again, with quite a different result.

Danny went overseas during World War II, and soon became the British Empire Flyweight Champion. All told, I think that he lost one bout while he was overseas in England, and this loss occurred under questionable circumstances, because Danny maintained that he had been drugged by his handlers. After he returned from serving overseas, Danny fought as a lightweight, and ultimately became the Canadian lightweight champion. Eventually, a fight was set up between him and Johnny Greco. Greco proved to be too strong for him, and stopped Danny in the 5th round. He did likewise to Ralph Walton, in a fight that took place in Montreal's Exchange Stadium.

Encouraged by the success of Al Evans, Ralph Walton and especially of Danny Webb, other lesser lights from Little Burgundy tried their hand at boxing, but none of them succeeded. Usually these untrained or marginally-trained aspirants, would sign up for a fight in one of Quebec's hinterlands, such as Shawinigan Falls or Thetford Mines for example. There they would encounter a local tough who had limited boxing skills, but who could punch like the kick of a mule. The inevitable result was that the would-be 'boxer' from Little Burgundy would end up flat on the ring mat.

But there were other people in Little Burgundy who were worth saying something about. They were about seven American men (from the Southern United States) who came to Montreal, to work as Porters on the Canadian Nation Railway. I don't remember exactly how or why they came. All I know for sure is that they did come. And more importantly, is that at least one of them made and continues to make a contribution to Canada, through one of his offsprings. That individual's name is Preston Jennings, who came to Montreal from Birmingham, Alabama in the late 1940s. Before I elaborate on how Preston's offspring contributes to Canada, let me say a word about his fellow émigrés. Five of them became exemplary residents (and in some cases) citizens of Canada. But two did not. One came here having allegedly abandoned his spouse back home in the USA, and became (or more probably continued to be) a notorious woman-beater. One day, he tried to start a conversation with me. When I ignored him, he said to me '. . . Oh Nigger, you think that you're so great because you went to college'. With that, I turned to him and said '. . . Lonnie, if you mess with me, you'll find that I'm not a women!' He never ever pursued the matter further.

The other started out to be a fun-loving guy, but later became a thug (and a hit-man) for one of the local unions. Now back to Preston Jennings and his family.

Preston and his wife (Gilberte) had six daughters and two sons. One daughter Marlene is a member of the House of Commons, having been elected as the Liberal member for Notre Dame de Grace—Lachine (Quebec) in 1997, 2000, 2004 and 2006. She graduated as a lawyer (LLB) from UQAM in 1986, and was called to the Quebec bar in 1988. Since February 2006, she has been the Deputy House Leader for the Official Opposition.

One of Marlene's brothers (Preston Jennings jr.) graduated from Concordia University in 1979(B.Comm; MBA). Subsequently, he was employed as the General Supervisor of Operations Analysis for a major Automobile manufacturer in Oshawa (ON).

For his part, Preston was particularly active in Mount Moriah Lodge No.24. He also served the fledgling Porter's Union (The International Brotherhood of Sleeping Car Porters) as secretary-treasurer, before his untimely death at age 66 in January 1981.

So not only was Preston a lover of children, and someone who cared about their education—he was also deeply committed to being a contributing part of the institutions in his adopted community.

There is another individual that I admired for his general service to the community, even though it was not the sort of activity that usually brings accolades to the person doing it. He was a self employed deliverer of ice (in the summer months), and someone who would move you on Montreal's traditional moving day, May 1st. His name was Mr. Franklin, and he did this by pulling a somewhat oversized, self-made handcart, for many miles each day, around Little Burgundy's streets.

He wore a pair of shoes, the heels of which were so acutely cut, that he always seemed to be walking on the outer sides of his heels. But this did not hamper him from walking many miles each day, while carrying out his ice delivery or moving chores—nor did it hamper his reliability. Whatever he undertook to do, he could be relied upon to do it.

He was not a very big man, but he was unbelievably strong. During the several times that he moved our family (from one dwelling to another), he never had a helper, yet he lifted and delivered every piece of furniture that we had. I never knew whether or not there was a Mrs. Franklin, but I understand that he had a son, James.

After many years of self-employment, Mr. Franklin retired. For several years, I saw him nattily attired (and with nice-fitting shoes), walking near to my home in 'Little Burgundy'. Then suddenly, I never saw him again. Evidently he had passed on—essentially unnoticed and unsung. But he'll always be someone that I'll admire, because he asked nothing of life but to be of service to the community. And that he delivered that in spades.

There were other 'Little Burgundy' residents that I regard as heroes, because they were committed to seeing that their children got an education, far in excess of their own. Today's youngsters have no appreciation of how difficult it was to do so back then. I am referring to the late 1930s to say the end of World War II in 1945. With the possible exception of scholars from the Caribbean, blacks (and especially those who were native born) were systematically discouraged from seeking higher education. And if a black dared to go on, the omnipresent problem was, who was going to hire you? Yet despite this real prospect of futility hanging over their head, some of our parents persisted in educating their children, or instilling the determination in their children to pursue this goal.

As we read in the bible (John I, 46) Nathanael said to Philip . . . 'Can any good thing come out of Nazareth?' Philip said to him '. . . Come and see'.

A similar question could have been raised about the then residents of Little Burgundy. But without fear of contradiction, I am prepared to answer yes, unequivocally—for there are many examples that I can cite, in support of this affirmation.

I am now going to list some former residents of Little Burgundy who went on to achieve noteworthy success in their post-secondary education.

Now the list of people that I am going to designated as 'heroes' is by no means all-inclusive, and for the most part they lived in 'Little Burgundy' for nearly all of their early adult years. And while I will name the actual person that I am designating, I am also lauding their parents for having the foresight to encourage their children to seek higher education.

One of the first of my heroes is the late Louise Daniel Lewis, who was one of the first

Black females to obtain a Bachelor of Arts degree from Sir George Williams College in 1943. She was the daughter of Mr. and Mrs. Orthni Daniel. Another is Kathleen Bramble Daly, who graduated from St. Mary's Hospital in 1951, and is reported to be the first black nurse to have graduated and worked as such in Montreal. Her sister Rosalyn (now Mrs. Roslyn Bramble-Adams) obtained a B.Sc. from Sir George Williams University in 1955. They lived on Richmond Square (with their mother, who came from the Caribbean island of Montserrat) in their youth. Other Richmond Square dwellers (who went on to earn university degrees) were brothers Harold and Calvin Potter, and sisters Lucille and Mairuth (Vaughan). All of them went on to distinguished careers, both in academia and elsewhere in the work-a-day world.

Two more of my Little Burgundy honourees lived on Lusignan St. They were Thamis Gale and Roy Rogers. What both had in common was that they were veterans of World War II, who had taken advantage of demobilization benefits to further their education. Roy went on to earn a Chemical Engineering degree from McGill University, and Thamis earned a B.Sc. in physics from Sir George Williams University. Both went on to do creditable work in their chosen fields.

There is another family that I would like to salute. They also lived on Lusignan St., and were then known as the Taylor family. I attended High School with Bennie, a brother of the family that I want to single out. They left Montreal for the United States, many years ago.

Why, I have no idea. But recently they returned to Montreal, as the Sandoval family. And two of the girls in the family had acquired post-graduate degrees in the USA. The older sister Corliss earned a Master's degree, while her younger sister Dolores, obtained a Ph.D. Dolores (who is an Emeritus professor from the

University of Vermont) continues to beneficially impact many aspects life, for both blacks and whites in Montreal. Indeed, both Corliss and Dolores are a credit to Little Burgundy.

And finally, I would like to offer a tribute to my late mother, who always championed education in our home, while functioning as a single mother since the death of my father in 1931. Five of her six children graduated from High School—and two went on to earn university degrees.

Some of Little Burgundy's home-grown icons were jazz musicians. Three who come to mind are the Sealey brothers—Hugh, George and Milton. The two older brothers (Hugh and George) played the saxophone, and both were regarded as better than average. And the youngest brother Milton, was a pianist. In fact, in the late 1940s, there were three great black jazz pianists domiciled in Little Burgundy. Unofficially, they were ranked as follows. The incomparable Oscar Peterson was designated

'The King', Oliver Jones was considered to be 'The Duke' and Milton Sealey was regarded as 'The Viscount'.

But there were a number of other indigenous jazz musicians worth mentioning, because two of them performed at Little Burgundy's two nightclubs. Allan Wellman was a great trumpet player, who was a regular at Rockhead's Paradise, while Harold (Steep) Wade was a saxophonist at the Ste. Michel cabaret. And Bill Kersey (a saxophonist), Bob Rudd (a bassist) and Charles Biddle (also a bassist)—all of whom came from the United States, were itinerant jazz musicians who also played in Little Burgundy.

Subsequently, Biddle achieved fame as the creator of Montreal's International Jazz Festival and for opening Biddle's Jazz and Ribs restaurant, also in Montreal.

However, jazz was not the only thing that Little Burgundy was infamous for.

There was a minor amount of prostitution, and some marijuana use, primarily by one person. I'll exclude naming her, because in my view she was more to be pitied than scorned. Her typical way of soliciting a client was to stand in a doorway on St. Antoine St. (just west of Mountain St.), high on marijuana, awaiting an offer for her sexual favours. I remember a white merchant mariner, who emerged from an encounter with her, exclaiming loudly '. . . Wow, and I thought that I had left the Great Lakes!'

Speak-easies were also commonplace. These were places where you could buy literally bathtub liquor after hours, and also indulge your sexual appetite for a modest fee.

And in a kind of reversed pedophilia, some older women solicited teen-age boys and young men, to satisfy their sexual needs. One such woman was a Mrs. Harrington. I had heard of her proclivity in this regard, but I had never experienced it. That was soon to change. It was a Sunday afternoon, and my younger brother Michael and I were standing near to the Snack Shop, on St. Antoine St. Mrs. Harrington and a lady friend of hers drove up in her car, and stopped near to where we were standing. She asked us if we were Mrs. Massiah's sons. When we affirmed that we were, she asked us if we would like to go for a drive in her car. Now in those days, a drive in anyone's car was a noteworthy event, so we gladly accepted the offer. But the ride unfolded somewhat differently than we expected, and we found ourselves being driven through the port area of Montreal, loaded with scores of merchant ships. Evidently Mrs. Harrington knew where she was going, because she made her way unerringly to one of the moored ships. She stopped her car, got out, boarded the ship, and was gone for perhaps 15 to 20 minutes. I have no idea what was the purpose of her visit to the ship (although I suspect that drugs were involved), and Michael and I provided camouflage as being part of a nice family, out for a Sunday drive. When she resumed the drive, she suggested that we go to an out-of-the-way bar in Montreal's Bout de L'Ile. I had no problem with this, and since she was providing the drive, I decided that Michael and I would pay for the drinks. Well shortly after the first round of drinks, Mrs. Harrington suggested that the four of us should repair to a motel in Chambly, '. . . to have some fun . . .' as she put it. Thereupon, I informed her that my fiancée would be joining me later that Sunday (from Chambly), and that Michael and I would take a cab back to Montreal, if she felt disinclined to drive us back to town! Well to her credit, she did drive us back to town, but at speeds around 75mph. And happily, this was my one and only encounter with Mrs. Harrington.

Eventually, there was a decline in cabarets in Little Burgundy, and they were replaced by two bars, just slightly North of Rockheads and the Ste. Michel. Thus the Casablanca Bar was opened on Mountain St. just North of what was Dorchester St. (now Boulevard René Levesque), and the Esquire Show Bar opened around the corner, on Stanley St.

Chapter 4

CHERISHED BELIEFS AND
OTHER QUIRKS
OF
LITTLE BURGUNDY

One of the things that never ceased to amaze me about the place that I inhabited during the formative years of my youth, was the status attributed to one's supposed sexual prowess. You were considered to be some sort of superman, if you claimed to be proficient in bed, even though such proficiency was never actually demonstrated. Regrettably, I never shared one of my favourite thoughts with those who held such views. It is this. Anatomically, the head of humans is placed higher than the genitalia. Therefore it is reasonable to conclude that it should have a higher priority than one's gonads. And one should also note that an amoeba (which is a singled cell protozoa) can also procreate. So why should you feel like 'Mr. Big', just because you impregnated some woefully uninformed female?

I heard a fellow named John boast '. . . man, I had that bitch in bed, naked as she was born!' As far as I remember, John never graduated from High School. But he was proud to boast of his supposed competence in bed!

Another characteristic of Little Burgundy was that it was a place where the n-word was used liberally. And there were so many pithy saying used to make a point. One that comes to mind is '. . . Nigger, just because you face is black and your lips are red, does not mean that your mouth is a prayer book!'. Or '. . . Nigger, I'll whip your ass just as sure as there is a hound in Texas, and you know that Dallas is nothing but a puppy town!'. Intimidation was rampant in Little Burgundy, and if you succumbed to it once, you would be victimized forever. The thing was to call the intimidator's bluff. I saw this done dramatically one day in Rockhead's tavern.

A chap named Bill, verbally accosted a fellow named Marcel, saying repeatedly to him, '. . . Cel, I know that I can whip you!'. This went on for several minutes, and each time the threat became louder. Finally, Marcel became exasperated by Bill's ranting, and invited him to step outside. With that, Bill cowered, saying to Marcel '. . . Cel, can't you take a joke? I was only kidding!'. Thereafter, I never heard Bill utter a threatening word to anyone. He was silenced forever. And so it was with other would-be toughs. If you stood up to them, invariably they backed down. One fellow I knew summarized his disdain for these so-called 'bad guys' by saying that the only thing 'bad' about them, was that they smelled bad!.

As I alluded to earlier, in telling about the character of Little Burgundy, it was a place where so-called hep-cats prevailed. These were primarily the fellows who were with it so to speak, in terms of their ability to dance, and also in their egregious attire.

Zoot suits were fashionable in the 1940s, but not only in the black community. So let me describe what constituted a typical zoot suit. Everything about them was exaggerated. The jacket was long enough to reach the knees, and the shoulders were padded at least 4 inches on each side. And the trousers rose to just below one's chest, with knees typically 32 inches circumferentially, tapering down to a 12 to 14 inch cuff.

Now these suits provoked anger, especially among members of Canada's navy, who wore bell-bottomed trousers as part of their uniform. They regarded all zoot-suiters as being draft-dodgers, in a nation that was at war. So they took it upon themselves to humiliate and harass zoot-suiters wherever and whenever they encountered them. It was not uncommon for two sailors to grab a zoot-suiter, and literally rip his suit off his back! Usually the assault took place at one of Montreal's many dance halls, and the victim never had a chance to protect his suit or himself. Nor were the perpetrators ever punished. Now I don't recall any black zoot-suitors being assaulted, but as a group, we reckoned that it was only a matter of time before our turn to be attacked would come. So we made some preparations for what we felt was an inevitability.

Up till then in my life, I had never carried a knife or razor on my person, and I never wore a zoot-suit. But I did wear peg-bottom trousers, and I was black. In addition, I had a part-time job at a florist on Mountain St., just North of the Naval Headquarters that was also on Mountain St. So whenever I went to work at the Florist's shop, I had to pass the Naval Headquarters. Given the hostility of the sailors to zoot-suiters, I felt threatened, even though no sailor ever said anything to me, and as I said earlier, I never wore a zoot-suit.

Nevertheless, I decided to take out some insurance by arming myself with a razor. At the time, I had an older cousin who was in the Canadian army. I asked him if he had a straight razor that I could borrow. He said yes that he did have a spare razor, so I asked him to let me borrow it. When I got it, I sharpened it by stropping it on the leather sharpener used for that purpose. Then I camouflaged it behind a handkerchief that I wore in my suit jacket's breast pocket. Thus armed, I felt secure when I walked past the Naval Headquarters. Happily, I never had to use the razor to protect myself from sailors or anyone else at that time. The closest we came to an encounter with sailors, occurred one evening when some 20 or so of us were gathered (for no discernible purpose) on St. Antoine St., just West of Mountain St. Suddenly, a truckload of sailors (equipped with belaying pins) drove up Mountain St, and stopped at the corner of St. Antoine St. With that, all the blacks (who were standing on St. Antoine St.) bared a variety of knives and razors that they had concealed up till then, and awaited what they anticipated would be an attack by the sailors. However, when the sailors viewed what awaited them, one of the sailors in the truck yelled to the driver . . . . **'no zoot-suiters here!'**. And just as suddenly as they had appeared, the sailors drove away. To the best of my awareness, that was the first and last time that sailors attempted to attack blacks in Little Burgundy. With that, I stopped carrying the razor that I had borrowed from my cousin, and I have never carried one again.

Throughout the time that I lived in Little Burgundy, there were some things that I never understood. One was the penchant of black porters for gambling, and in particular with each other. As is known, most (if not all) of the black men worked as porters for one of the three railroads that operated out of Montreal. And their take-home pay was meager. Yet many of these porters would spend much of their leisure time betting on the races, or gambling at the Elks Lodge, against each other. I remember something that had a lifelong impact on me. It involved my father. As some of you may know, I lost my father in 1931, when I was nearly 5 years old. But I remember my Dad coming home one day, turning his pants pockets inside out, and saying to my mother, '. . . Mae, the ponies ran out!'. From that Day, I made a vow that I would never gamble on the horses (or anything else for that matter) and I have kept that vow to this day.

So as I said earlier, there are things that I have never been able to understand about so many of the black men that I encountered, while living in Little Burgundy. It seems that most of them had no meaningful goals in life. They had a job on the railroad, that unfortunately led nowhere for most of them. And they seemed to accept this as their due, by occupying themselves endlessly in the pursuit of purposeless activities, such as gambling and debauchery.

One day I met a fellow named Jimmy who was just two months younger than me. But, unlike me, he had become one of the noted gamblers in Little Burgundy. However, on this particular day I saw him banging his head repeatedly against one of the metal hydro-electric poles, and saying .... 'why didn't I know when to quit?' He stopped banging his head against the pole long enough to explain his plight. He had won $950 at the table where he was gambling, and decided that he wanted to top it off by winning $1000. Instead, he went on to lose every dollars that he had won. Thus his attempt at self-mutilation. His experience and that of my Father (that I related earlier), reinforced my life-long aversion to gambling. If only this aversion would afflict more black men, and especially the preponderance of low-wage-earners among them.

Chapter 5

THE TREADMILL

Rockhead's tavern was undoubtedly the locus of what I chose to call the place where you could find those who were trapped in the perpetually non-productive aspects of life in Little Burgundy. Invariably whenever you frequented the tavern, you would be challenged with a seemingly important question, of absolutely no importance to anyone but the questioner. For instance, one would be asked, which is the bigger snake, a boa constrictor or an anaconda? Even if you knew the answer, of what importance was it, since it is highly unlikely that the questioner will ever see either of these reptiles. Another favourite question involved the dice—game of craps. The question would ask, '. . . supposed you made twenty passes, starting with a dollar, and doubled up each time. Would you end up with a million dollars? Whenever I was asked this question (and I was asked it many times), I would tell the questioner that there were two answers. Yes, $1.00, doubled 20 times would generate just over $1 million dollars—actually $1,048, 575 to be exact. But I also told the questioner that he wouldn't have the nerve to stick it out through twenty passes! These are but two of the many mind-numbing queries that one would encounter on a daily basis in this environment.

The stultifying effect of being endlessly involved in the nonsensical ramblings that went on in Little Burgundy, (on a daily basis) certainly took its toll. And increasingly it became virtually impossible to hear a worthwhile utterance there. So whenever I chanced upon one of the more vociferous of her residents, I knew what to expect.

Almost beside Rockhead's tavern was a restaurant whose patrons were largely the same as those who patronized Rockhead's. But their tactics were slightly different. Invariably they would leave the restaurant for a brief period, then return, and ask—what happened? It was just as though they expected something cataclysmic to happen, during their brief absence.

And since it never did happen, they continued to ask—what happened?

Another of the characters that were part of Little Burgundy in those days was the MC at Rockhead's Paradise. His stage name was Alonzo Hunt. One day, a local prostitute sought his advice regarding money that she was giving to her pimp. She told Alonzo that he was never satisfied with her earnings. Alonzo's advice to her was as follows. 'Ho, if today you bring $20.00, tomorrow bring $40.00. If you bring

$40.00 one day, next day bring $80.00. Ho . . . always bring mo!'

But there were also non-blacks who frequented Little Burgundy. One was a Jewish fellow, who was called Rosie. He made no bones about being gay. One day, I was on the # 49 streetcar with a chap from Haiti, when Rosie boarded the tram. I told the fellow from Haiti about Rosie being gay. Then I greeted Rosie, and asked him how he was. He replied that he was not feeling all that great, because he was having his period! After a lapse of about 5 minutes, Rosie approached me saying '. . . Hi babe, would you like to go somewhere to have some fun?' I assured Rosie that I had no interest in engaging in 'fun' with him, or any other man. Thereupon he dismissed me saying '. . . Ok, Baby stay freakish if you want to!'. This is but one of many bizarre happenings that I experienced during the time that I lived in that locale.

Chapter 6

THE VANGUARDS COME TO TOWN

My late younger brother Michael felt that Black-oriented social activities in Montreal had declined almost to the point of non-existence, when even the perennial New Years matinee, put on by the Coloured Woman's Club, was discontinued in the early 1950s. So in 1959, he recruited five of his friends (Roland Wills, Alfred Braithwaite, Marcus Durant, Edson Ford, Reggie Cumberbatch) and me, to form a social activities club. At the time, I had just started work on my doctorate at L'Université de Montréal, and had no desire to be part of such a club. But for some reason, Michael wanted me aboard, and even paid my initial fee to assure my participation in his fledgling club. Each member had to put in $50.00, to provide start-up capital for the club. This fee would be returned to each member from the proceeds of the club's first successful social venture.

The name Vanguard was chosen deliberately. It was meant to signify a group at the forefront of a movement. In the case of the Vanguards, the movement was the revitalization of social events in Montreal's Black community.

Our operational method was deceptively simple. We decided to use the existing facts. Clearly more than 90% of Montreal's Black male breadwinners worked for one of the three railways operating out of the city. And these railways had one thing in common.

Members of the Vanguards

From left: Edson Ford, Tom Massiah, Reggie Cumberbatch, Michael Massiah, Roland Wills, Marcus Durant, Alfred Braithwaite

It was that they had a bi-weekly payday, that was always on a Thursday. So we always scheduled our dances for the Friday immediately after payday. They were held at the Rialto Hall, on Park Avenue, near to Hutchison Street. Our dance motif was that we provided continuous music, by hiring two bands—one that played swing music and the other was a calypso band. Early in our operations we determined that more than 80% of our revenue was derived from the bar. So our strategy was to attract and retain a minimum of 200 patrons at our dances. We did so primarily by keeping the admission fee reasonably low, and by selling both beer and liquor at reasonable prices. But our most inventive undertaking was to provide barbecued chicken (from the Swiss Chalet Barbecue) which we sold to the patrons essentially at our cost. We brought in the chicken around 12:30 a.m. to prevent the usual exodus of attendees to Chinatown, for some Chinese food. At first, some of our patrons expressed no interest in buying the chicken dinners that we were providing. But soon, as the inviting odours permeated the dancehall, we had no trouble in selling every chicken that we had ordered. But more importantly, we had retained our attendees, which did wonders for our bar earnings.

One might think that we would encounter problems with some of our more rambunctious patrons, because of the amount of beer and liquor being consumed at our dances. But we never did. As soon as we spotted potential trouble, the three off-duty Vanguards would converge unobtrusively around the individual, speak quietly to him or her (assuring them that we knew that they wanted to have a good time at our dance), and placating them with a complimentary drink of their choice. It worked every time.

We held only one formal event and that took place at l'Université de Montréal's Cercle Universitaire, on Sherbrooke St. East. A feature of the dance was that we provided each attendee with a complementary five-pack of cigarettes, given them by an attractive young lady. Since many more people smoked in those days, than is true today, this added touch went over very well with the attendees.

As I stated earlier, The Vanguards were markedly community-oriented.

So one of the first things that we did (once we had sufficient funds in our account), was to supply some Christmas hampers to needy black families. We had hoped to be able to actually deliver the hampers to the families,

The Vanguards in Formal Wear

and approached the then Executive Director of the Negro Community Centre (Buster Clyke) for the name of twelve families who could use a

Christmas hamper. But he refused to give us any names. Instead, he told us to deliver the hampers to the NCC, and he would see that they would be delivered. Reluctantly, we agreed to this alternative, although we would definitely have preferred to deliver the hampers ourselves.

I undertook to procure the hampers, as I had access a Mr. Switchman, who was one of the senior managers of Steinberg's groceteria, on St. Catherine St., near to Guy St. When I told Mr. Switchman what I wanted, he called the store manger over to where I was, and instructed him to provide me with whatever I needed. In all, I was able to procure enough provisions to fill twelve hampers, and I paid considerably less than the actual price for what I had received. At the time I had a car with an enormous trunk, so I was able to get all of the hampers unto my car, using both the trunk and the back seat. Subsequently, I delivered the hampers to the NCC. Presumably they delivered them to the needy families of their choice. But I do not recall The Vanguards ever receiving an official acknowledgement of our gift from Buster Clyke or anyone else at the NCC.

We made another donation to the NCC, in the form of some gymnastic equipment that they claimed to need. But this time we insisted that either Buster Clyke or one of his representatives attend our dance, in order to receive our gift. It was not that we needed or wanted publicity for our gift. But we had heard that functionaries at the NCC were disparaging the Vanguards unjustifiably. So we hoped to dispel the negative things they had reportedly been saying about us, by having them actually attend one of our functions.

Ultimately, we decided to disband the Vanguards, because we had succeeded in restoring social activities in the Montreal black community. So without any great flourish on our part, we wound up activities as an events-sponsoring group.

Chapter 7

DÉNOUEMENT

So now you have a flavour of some of the things that occurred in Little Burgundy. I have tried to report accurately on as many of these occurrences as I can recall. But obviously I have omitted some of them. And there were other characters who were perhaps worth mentioning, but who were left out because they did not add significantly to the overall narrative. For instance, I didn't say anything about the Red Caps, who did back-breaking work, serving C.P.R. passengers, as they either boarded or disembarked from trains at Windsor Station. Several of them died from heart attacks, induced by lifting heavy bags, day-in and day-out, as part of their job with the C.P.R. While there is nothing that I want to say about each individual Red Cap I feel that I can pay tribute to them as a group, by giving a partial list of their names, Those whom I remember are Dudley Francis, Alfred Butler, George (Shine) Blackman, Thomas Terrelonge, Harold Thomas, Alfred Potter, Walter Morris, Clyde King, Norman Jones, Vernon Mahomed and Sydney Flood.

Moreover, at least one Red Cap, a Mr. Grant, diversified by becoming the owner of a rooming house (on St. Antoine St., near to Versailles St.), that he ran successfully for a number of years.

Other minor characters, not mentioned in the main narrative, include a fellow who had the sobriquet Dr. Waters, and another fellow Birdie Ash, who was also known as the Little Corporal. There was also a doorman called King Powell, who guarded access to Rockhead's Paradise for several years.

While each of the foregoing were indeed minor characters, I feel that my reportage on Little Burgundy would be incomplete, without saying something about them. So here goes. Dr. Waters acquired his moniker because of the fact that he could reconstitute a dry-gin bottle, (filled with water), so that it looked like the real thing. I don't know how many of these bogus bottles that he was able to sell to his unsuspecting marks, but evidently there were many, because he continued to do so for years.

I don't know much about Birdie Ash, except to say that he served overseas (in the Canadian army) during World War II, and reached the rank of a corporal. After he returned from serving overseas, he undertook to participate in some voter-intimidation activities, during municipal elections. On one of these ventures, he was shot in the buttocks, when he accidentally allowed his rear end to protrude beyond his cover. Thereafter, we had a great time imitating Birdie, as he tried to deflect the pain he experienced, on being shot in his behind.

King Powell was not an imposing figure as a doorman, because not only was he rather diminutive, but he was also fairly old when he undertook these duties. However, he made up for these deficiencies by being adept at cutting people with a straight razor. So, because of his reputation, (as a razor-wielding specialist), essentially no one messed with him. However, the last time that I saw King Powell, he was barely able to raise his arms, let alone defend himself. Shortly after that, he died, without causing even a ripple in the community.

What I have tried to portray are the peculiarities that made Little Burgundy the enticing place that it was. Now it no longer exists. All that remains is its corpse. I hope that in these few pages, I have done enough to make it worth remembering, as the exciting part that it was of that great city, Montreal.

EPILOGUE

Now while I have related things that occurred in the past, I want to caution the reader about looking back too much on the past. The past is only useful if one can learn from it. Remember that Santayana said '. . . Those who ignore the lessons of history, are bound to re-live them'. Therefore heed my admonition to let go of the past—except for its lessons.

Some time ago, I wrote a poem which emphasizes this advice. I will append it here at the end of my novel.

Let Go Of The Past:
by

Tom Massiah

As I went for a stroll the other day—
A voice deep within me seemed to say,
'Let go of the past, my oft—wounded son!
Your past hurts are over—they're
done, they're done!
You never can avenge oppressors of old,
For many are enfeebled, and some
are stone cold!'
You may have believed that
revenge satisfies,
But that view is true only for
misguided eyes.
The wisest course is to discard the load—
Get rid of all things that disturb
your abode!

Instead of remorse—think how
blessed you are,
To still be aware of each heavenly star.
So count not what you've lost
through the years,
But give thanks you can smile—
through all of your tears.
Be thankful as well that you still can show,
That your blessings exceed all your
sorrows and woe.